T0114782

the Miracle
Pollinate

Susan Farah

BALBOA.PRESS
A DIVISION OF HAY HOUSE

Balboa Press books may be ordered through booksellers or by contacting:

Balboa Press
A Division of Hay House
1663 Liberty Drive
Bloomington, IN 47403
www.balboapress.com
844-682-1282

Because of the dynamic nature of the Internet, any web addresses or links contained in this book may have changed since publication and may no longer be valid. The views expressed in this work are solely those of the author and do not necessarily reflect the views of the publisher, and the publisher hereby disclaims any responsibility for them.

The author of this book does not dispense medical advice or prescribe the use of any technique as a form of treatment for physical, emotional, or medical problems without the advice of a physician, either directly or indirectly. The intent of the author is only to offer information of a general nature to help you in your quest for emotional and spiritual well-being. In the event you use any of the information in this book for yourself, which is your constitutional right, the author and the publisher assume no responsibility for your actions.

Any people depicted in stock imagery provided by Getty Images are models, and such images are being used for illustrative purposes only. Certain stock imagery © Getty Images.

This book is a work of non-fiction. Unless otherwise noted, the author and the publisher make no explicit guarantees as to the accuracy of the information contained in this book and in some cases, names of people and places have been altered to protect their privacy.

Scripture quotations marked NIV are taken from the Holy Bible, New International Version®. NIV®. Copyright © 1973, 1978, 1984 by International Bible Society. Used by permission of Zondervan. All rights reserved. [Biblica]

Print information available on the last page.

ISBN: 979-8-7652-2736-7 (sc)
ISBN: 979-8-7652-2737-4 (e)

Balboa Press rev. date: 04/22/2022

This book is dedicated to Stacey –

May our legacies surpass our dreams...

Contents

Prologue

Do you know how important you are?

How incredibly significant and essential you are to the world? And how incredibly important you are to the lives of others?

We all are - every human being on this planet.

In fact, it's more than that. It's not just humans but every single creature on this planet - animal, fish, bird, insect and reptile.

Wait, I'll go a step further than that to include trees and plants and all things living in the ocean - basically every living thing.

But let's get back to you - the one who every day impacts the world and personally impacts the hundreds of individuals God clutters your path with each day.

Don't believe me? Don't believe it's true?

Too bad...

Because it is true and all you have to do to realize it is to pay attention the next time you go through a trial and come out the other side. Watch what happens next. Within weeks or maybe even days or hours God will put in your path someone who is going through that same trial. Or maybe they just went through that trial and are now suffering because of it and need *your* encouragement - a hand, a friend.

Why does God do that? He does it for you.

Why?

So, you can share with them what you went through and how God not only brought you through the trial but about the blessing that came out of that trial.

Because there always is a blessing you know; after the storm there is peace, after the rain there is a rainbow and after the dark night comes the next morning.

And joy... And since you are God's hands and feet here on earth, you are to be that word of wisdom; bridging the gap between them and God, bringing them closer together so healing can take place.

"I can do all that?" you are thinking. Absolutely!

But first, let's talk a little about *Proverb 25:11* - your instructions. Then we'll learn something about bees and why they are important and why we all should strive to "bee" exactly like the bees.

Chapter One

A word...

What is a word anyway?

The English Thesaurus defines it as a statement - a declaration.

I've heard of an opening statement as in a trial in a court of law, calculated and strategized - the first remarks given by both attorneys to grab the jury's attention and steal the show.

And I know we've all heard about a very important declaration - The Declaration of Independence which started this country on its road to freedom.

Sounds to me that *"a word"* is very significant and must be essential for changing things and bringing forth new information so somehing *can* change; circumstances, situations and people.

So, let me ask you, "When *you* speak and words come out of your mouth is that what they are doing - the words, I mean"?

Are your words making a difference?

Or are they just something to fill up the dead space - flying off your tongue and rambling on and on, not making a difference to anyone or anything.

Are they meaningful to others?

Or, are they just something spoken for your advantage; spoken so you can look good in front of others, spoken to make *you feel better about you.*

Are they spoken to win an argument so you can be on top and show your power over someone else?

Are they uplifting, encouraging and kind or deflating, damaging and cruel?

Are they words that can cause a person to miraculously walk on water or ones that will cause them to drown - swallowed up by a sea of negativity and hopelessness?

And these *"words of yours"* - where are they coming from? Are they coming from your heart?

And if you just answered that question with a "Yes", then what *is* in that heart of yours?

Is it an out-flowing of a loving relationship with God, (your Source) or is it resentment and anger from a life wasted on broken promises and unfulfilled hopes and dreams?

Are you a builder-upper or a "tearer-downer? Are you part of the problem or part of the solution?

If you really search your soul and answer these questions honestly you will discover how you feel about life, the world, God and yourself.

And until you do answer these questions you can't complete your purpose - your ultimate purpose for being here on earth at this precise moment in time.

I hope you *do* examine your thoughts and motives. It's important for you that you do because to truly help others you must first understand yourself.

But I do know one thing, you are searching- searching to be more, to do more, to be better than you are now - and to find answers. Maybe even to find the answer to the all-important question, "What am I supposed to do next?"

How do I know this? You are reading this book, right?

Oh, that's not the reason you say. It's because I was intrigued by the title or the "bee" was cute or I was bored or even something closer to the truth like. "I don't know- it just happened".

It happened because you are supposed to read it, there are no coincidences with God. Remember the Law of Attraction?

You and this book were drawn together; there are only realized intentions - realized, intended thoughts.

So now that you *have* chosen this book or *it* has chosen you and you have started reading it *and now* been challenged by me to examine yourself- you now have another choice.

The choice is, "What are you going to do about **it?**"

If you've decided that the words you speak are kind, uplifting and encouraging and you believe you have a loving relationship with God and basically go around "dogooding" every day of your life - then keep reading.

If you've decided that the words you speak are deflating, damaging and cruel *and* you have anger or resentment especially right now because I asked you to remind yourself of this - then keep reading this book.

Why?

Because this isn't just about words. We are not talking just about words here we are talking about "A Word".

"A Word"

A particular thing; *the* particular thing that is going to change lives, the thing that is going to move mountains - the very thing that will change a river to red, part a sea or resurrect a life.

Now that's *"A WORD"*.

Now some of you are thinking, "God doesn't want me to do that" or "I can't do that" or "He's never asked me to do that", or "I don't want to do that" or even - "Why *should* I do that".

It doesn't matter which one of these roadblocks, brick walls or stop signs you are trying to use to "not to have to" do the thing God wants you to do; they won't work forever.

Why?

Because God, (that which has no beginning and no end) always gets his way.

4

Or for those of you who might get a little twinge with the word "God" it's because "The Universe", "The Source" or whatever you call it or whatever name you choose to use to describe the entity that created you/us - *always get its way.*

So, get over it!

Get over the verbiage!

And another thing, get over the notion that you go through life *not* affecting others and that what you say and do only affects *you.* I hope you are not still holding on to that piece of denial and bringing it out when you don't want to do something.

I hope you are really not that naive or think that others are.

I'm not trying to hurt your feelings or ruffle your feathers but even if you try not to affect others - not doing will cause you to affect others the same as if you *did* do something.

In fact, your mere existence affects others. You can't get away from it so, you might as well, be good at it and *do good* with it.

But back to God (the Universe), always getting his "way". It's true!

No matter to what great lengths and for how long you resist the very thing that will change the lives of others, (and change your life, too) eventually you will give in.

Either you will finally get the truth of your purpose and start doing it or it will happen without you and you will die having missed the opportunity to be totally amazing.

Oh, you may be a little amazing - but you missed the "totally" amazing part.

Or, the someone who was chosen because you wouldn't do it, will do it and *they are living that totally amazing life that could have been yours.*

So, for all of you with a reason buzzing around your head that you can't, you don't want to or don't have time to fulfill your purpose and do *this thing* - again, get over it.

Now, let's get back to what's important - A Word.

In the context that the bible uses it, and in the context that we are going to use it here - it means enlightened message, not just a message. Not just a statement. Not just an, "off the cuff" comment, but "something the person you are saying it to - *needs* to hear".

And very importantly, this person does not need to hear it because *you* think they need to hear it. Because *you* know exactly what they need to hear and they are going to listen to you or else.

Why? Because *you* did not think this word up - it's enlightened, remember?

You are just the delivery system, very important - but not the originator of this word.

Since the message isn't from you it would not be something you normally would be rushing to tell them. It could be confusing or uncomfortable for them, but it's important and may change their life - if they let it.

It could be an answer to the prayer they have been praying for a long time. It could be the way to contact a person they must contact, maybe a doctor that will save their mother's life.

It could be a scripture that puts them back on the right path Or, it could be a name for their dog.

The point it - it's important for some reason and the task was given to you to do.

It's serious business, very serious business. It comes from beyond you - even though it is in your head, and you are the one saying it to them. The true meaning is just for them.

But you're the *one* - the one chosen. Why, you?

Well, because God has been preparing you to do it even if you don't realize it, silly.

"This vast universe has orchestrated people, places and things to prepare you so you can receive this "word" and deliver it. And another thing, the word must be *respected*. It needs your respect because much has been done to get it to you and to get you ready to do what you are about to do".

And because of all of that - it does not need you to stop the all-important flow of it.

It doesn't need you to mess it up.

You do not need to crush this message for any reason - not for fear and not because you don't understand it or understand why it is so important for that person to get it.

You may not understand it – but they do. Or they will.

The word will overtake them, consume them. It will roll around in their brain like a loose ball bearing until they figure it out - until they accept it.

Hey, but that isn't your concern. The only concern *you* have is to deliver the message and then - be quiet.

"Did you hear what I said?"

Be quiet…

Yes, it is not your job to interpret the word - that would make it all about you. And this word is not about you, remember - even though you are involved in the delivering - kinda like the UPS or Fed Ex guy.

The interpretation and ultimate responsibility of this enlightened message is theirs - not yours.

So, you must stay out of the way and not give them your opinion, try to sway them to think like you or to understand the message like you think you understand the message.

It's not about you - remember?

And once you have delivered the message (been obedient and done your part), they are now the one who is accountable to accept that word and do what is required of *them*.

What happens if you ignore your task - the task that has been given to you, the task that God thinks **you** must deliver because **you** are the perfect one to deliver it?

What happens is - **you lose and so do they.**

It's as simple as that.

Maybe they never receive the message because no one is willing to deliver it.

Maybe they don't receive the message because someone does decide to deliver it and they mess it up or the person won't accept it from *them*, (they weren't the perfect one like you were).

You lose because somewhere in the back of your mind you will always wonder - "What would have happened if I had delivered that message?" or "What happened because I didn't deliver that message?"

Either way it will haunt you. It will be pulled out at a moment at your weakest moment when you are down or discouraged or doubting yourself.

Then poof!

It is there in front of you. The thing *not done* - the thing left undone, making you miserable.

Why put yourself through that? It will be much worse than delivering the message in the first place.

Remember, whatever you chose - *you have to live with the consequences.*

So, if you are not thrilled, excited and full of anticipation to deliver the "word" get over it.

Get some gratitude, bathe in gratitude - be bold and courageous and obey that thought and turn it into action. Create that action, manifest it into reality - then stand back and see what happens.

In other words - *be part of the miracle.*

Your work to do: For the next 2 days journal – Day #1

_____

_____

_____

_____

_____

_____

_____

_____

_____

_____

_____

_____

_____

_____

_____

Day #2

Okay – look back at your two days of journaling. What do your words say?

What to your words say about you?

_____

_____

_____

_____

_____

_____

_____

_____

_____

_____

_____

_____

_____

_____

What did you discover? Would you do or say anything different? Whose life/lives did you affect?

_____

_____

_____

_____

_____

_____

_____

_____

_____

_____

_____

_____

_____

_____

Chapter Two

Aptly Placed...

Aptly - I really like the sound of this word, almost sounds like a happy word. It's musical but also proper-sounding - like an English (British), word. "It was aptly placed, Governor-· ta ta".

And then there is placed - positioned.

Positioned, not thrown out of a speeding car or dropped from the side of a cliff or even dumped out of a plane - but "po-si-tion-ed".

Last chapter we discovered the importance of "a word" which is that "a word" is critical - something that *must* be told to someone by somebody. And if you are the chosen one you better do it or that someone will suffer, you will suffer or someone else will be chosen and they will receive *your* blessing, again you suffer.

So, the message is very important - but not *all important*.

It's not *all* important because at this point it's really just words, until:

The right person at the right time in the right place with the right attitude and intentions delivers it and then shuts up. And lets the person they told the message to hear it, hopefully receive it, hopefully understand it, then accept it and do what they are supposed to do with it.

"Whew, that was a long sentence!"

And ...

"That's a lot of things that have to happen."

Well, right now it's not our job to worry about that, it's our job to talk about; "aptly placed".

We've said that placed is about positioning - setting it where it needs to be - not just plopped down anywhere, in any condition.

How about aptly?

Aptly is part of this all-important equation. And a very critical part of it because is "the where" of it.

The word just can't be delivered just anywhere you know.

I mean the destination is "the someone" but, "aptly" helps ensure they are in a position to hear it - this is crucial to "that someone". In fact, it could make all the difference between success and failure.

Aptly says that the message goes appropriately, correctly, properly and fittingly *and* placed to make sure it is intentional - that it has <u>intention</u> to it. That it is thought-out, deliberate, on purpose and planned.

Wow, that's a lot to make sure of - to be responsible for. And remember this is the part we *are* responsible for *and* accountable for, (whether we decide to do this thing or not).

Hmmm ...

Again, I can hear the wheels turning in your head and maybe even your stomach churning a little.

Nervous?

Realization that the blah, blah, blah we say to people isn't just blah, blah, blah - but something they make take to heart and act on, change their life because of it or hang the rest of their life on it.

So, all conversations are important?

You better believe it, buddy.

Why do you think God gave us two eyes, two ears and only one mouth?

You think he just ran out of material?

Or,

Do you think it's to see and hear twice as much as we speak?

Or,

Better still, only speak half of what we've *seen and heard to be true?*

Take the next ten minutes and really think about what you just read.

Susan Farah

Ahhh... Bingo!

Sounds to me like we should be doing a lot more of "being quiet" and a lot less of the blah, blah, blah. Ya think?

Everything we say and do affects others. Can I get an AMEN to that?

Now back to the message which was given to you but doesn't *mean anything to you* but means something *only to the person who you are supposed to deliver it to.*

That message, *the* message - the all-important message that must be given correctly. The message given in the right intention and delivered - exactly placed, (with intention).

That's right, intention - and all it implies; with meaning, purpose, objective, goals, a target and - a plan.

Well, we know there is a goal and it is to get it to the right person, at the right place and at the right time.

We know it will have meaning for *them* and there is a purpose and an objective to what we are doing, (even if we're not totally sure what they are).

And lastly - there must be a plan.

But how do we know what the plan is?

How do we carry out the plan if we don't understand what it all means?

Don't worry - it's not our plan - it's God's plan.

It's not ours so we don't have to worry about the plan - we're just the pizza delivery guy, right?

We just need to deliver.

But *what we do need to worry about* is staying tuned in and in-tune with God on a daily basis so we can *know to be at the right place, at the right time and talking to the right person.*

Because if we're not, then we could be pulling our pizza truck up to the wrong house, or delivering the wrong pizza to the right house or delivering the right pizza to the right house three hours late.

Any way you look at it, "We blew it!"

Oh, by the way - who says this delivery we are making has to be something we say, some long speech or even a scripture - not me.

Let me give you two perfect examples of messages that were not what we would call messages at all. They both involve my brother-in-law, Georgie.

Now Georgie was born different due to lack of oxygen at birth. He had terrible seizures as a baby and as a child and adult developmentally slow - but very special.

I met him as an adult, of course and soon was in awe of his uniqueness. And it's now my pleasure to share Georgie with you. Georgia lived with my husband and I for about a year and during that time on several occasions I witnessed Proverbs 25:11 in action.

Georgie loves ice cream so he and I went to the local ice cream shop, a wonderful place full of sweet treats and 25 flavors of home-made ice cream - it was great!

A married couple from our church owned the shop and the atmosphere was always uplifting. But on that particular day it seemed unusually quiet almost solemn and except for Tim behind the counter there was just one customer, sitting alone at the back table.

After Georgie and I decided what kind of ice cream cone we wanted and as I was talking to Tim I realized Georgie had drifted away from me. I turned around and he was standing beside the man at the table, touching him on his shoulder.

Now we never knew how new people might react to Georgie so I hurried over to make sure everything was okay. The man was kind and smiled at me and at Georgie and nodded his head to let me know there was no problem. After a few minutes it was time to go and as we walked out the door with cones in hand, Georgie waved good-bye with the biggest grin on his face.

I never gave the episode another thought until three weeks later when I stopped in that shop after work to pick up a dessert and Tim, the same young clerk who waited on me the last time, was there. As I walked in the door he called out to me and in an excited rush of words blurted out, "You'll never guess what happened!"

Of course, I had no way of knowing what to guess, so I said, "What?"

He proceeded to tell me the story about the customer at the table who Georgie had met. The gentleman was someone he and the owners knew well, (let's call him John). Over the years John had overcome many hardships in his life but had great resilience and was always able to rise above them. However, on that particular day when Georgie and I came in the shop he was going through a very, very difficult time and his friends were worried for him because he hadn't been able to pull out of this one.

Tim said after we left that day John left too and no one heard from him for several days until suddenly he showed up at the ice cream shop all smiles, laughing and making jokes with everyone there. He was happier and more out-going than they had ever seen him - it was as if a personality transplant had taken place.

He confided in Tim that after Georgie had touched his shoulder that day and looked into his eyes and smiled - something changed in him. He said that almost immediately he felt something different than he ever felt before. He couldn't exactly explain it. It wasn't just that he felt better, he felt happy. But it was more than happy even though happy had been something he hadn't felt in years.

This happy was better than the glimpses of happy he had experienced before.

This happy stayed and brought joy with it then later peace showed up too!

John asked Tim to be sure to tell me what had happened and how grateful he was that Georgie changed his life that day. He believed it was a miracle and I should never be afraid or try to stop Georgie from passing on God's love to someone.

John needed me to know what Georgie had done.

Not only had he changed his life, but he showed him God's love by exchanging sadness for love - depression for <u>unconditional</u> love.

WOW!

About two weeks after that Georgie and I were in the grocery store picking up a few items for supper. Georgie sometimes pushed the cart for me but sometimes he liked to walk a little ahead of me "to check things out".

We were in the diary aisle and as I turned to grab a carton of milk I heard Georgie say, "You're pretty".

I turned around and Georgie was standing next to a middle-aged woman who wasn't, (in my opinion) pretty. In fact, when I caught the first glimpse of her I thought, "Boy, she looks old for her age and *"not* happy".

But then something strange happened, the woman began to change. The first thing she did was smile, then she stood up straighter and her body began to look younger. The closer I got to her I realized the wrinkles I thought she had on her face were gone and her complexion began to take on a glow.

Yes, she was actually glowing!

As we passed each other, she smiled at me and softly whispered, "Thank you".

When she did this to my astonishment I realized she wasn't old at all. She wasn't middle-aged either. She was young - at the most thirty years old.

She had only looked old, weary and sad.

Seriously, in less than a minute - 20 years had disappeared from her face and body. A young woman now stood where an old woman had stood just minutes earlier.

Again, there had been a transplant.

A physical transplant this time - it was a true metamorphosis, just as if a new person had replaced the old one. A moth had just turned into a butterfly. Whatever had been in charge of her controlling her life disappeared and the "aptly – placed" touch (message), from God through Georgie had transformed her.

Words from a pure heart...

Just two simple words - but spoken by someone who just obeyed his heart and let God work through him.

Georgie, who did not have the capacity to conger up reasons why *not* to do it.

God placed it in his heart - he obeyed and God did the miracle.

Georgie - the right person in the right place, at the right time with the right person; "*a word aptly place*".

Perfect...

Now let's talk about the "imperfect".

Arguments - do you know why arguments are bad? Things fly out that you don't want to fly out.

So, what do we have?

Wrong place, wrong time, wrong intent and wrong message - we have the exact opposite of what God wants.

Haven't you ever just known you needed to tell someone something which may be hard for them to hear or even something you needed to get off your chest?

Better still. It's something you believe God wanted you to tell them?

But what happens?

You look for the opportune time, you wait, you plan and after all this waiting an argument happens. And then, "ZING" - out pops the message and all hell breaks loose.

You delivered the right message that you were holding on to for the perfect time and then - you delivered it at the worst possible moment.

You just wasted it.

In fact, not only did you waste it but the situation just moved two steps back from where it was - now making it harder for God to do what he needed to do for them and for you.

You just made God's job harder.

What happened?

Did you wait too long?

And since it was still there in your brain when it should have already been delivered and producing abundant harvest, you blew it!

Was it just an accident that it flew out and spoiled everything?

Or something more sinister - did your subconscious want everything to be ruined?

Were you afraid or being stubborn?

Was there something about the receiver you didn't like?

Did you not really want them to get the message and the blessing God wanted them to get?

Did you think they didn't deserve it or was it that you wanted to serve it the way YOU thought it should be served and so you manipulated circumstances until you could deliver a "knife" instead of a "word"?

Maybe you are innocent and just messed up.

So many possibilities - so many excuses. So many truths - so many reasons why the human race is so messed up.

The lesson here - never deliver a package if you are angry, unless God specifically asks you to do so.

Wouldn't it be great if we were all like Georgie - a touch, a smile, a compliment; easy ones.

But the reality is someone has to deliver the other ones - the "I need to get your attention" ones and the "What the heck are you doing" ones and the "Wake up and smell the roses" ones *before the recipient can't smell the roses because they are "pushing up daises".*

So, what have we learned my friend?

We must make it a priority to grow our relationship with God and listen – and, *"pay attention"*, to *his* side of the conversation so we will be ready.

Ready like it says in the bible - ready like the bride waiting for her bridegroom with oil in her lamp, *prepared.*

Faith... Trust... Belief... Obedience... TRUTH

Work to do: Think back and remember the times you felt you had very important messages to deliver. How did it go? What happened?

Were they aptly placed and received?

_____

_____

_____

_____

_____

_____

_____

_____

_____

_____

_____

_____

_____

How about the things you didn't say or do? What happened to those people?

_____

_____

_____

_____

_____

_____

_____

_____

_____

_____

_____

_____

_____

Chapter Three

Sound Illogical Or Impractical?

Sound impossible?

Then it must be God. Have you noticed that?

If you have been paying close attention in your life and the world around you - you will have realized this already, "God uses the impractical to amaze the practical and do some of his biggest miracles".

Why, you say.

So that it will be obvious to even the doubters that it was "more" than *that* person - it had to be because it was too big for a mere person to accomplish.

It had to be God - Our Source, the Alpha and Omega, the all-encompassing Universal Energy.

But a touch and a smile and just two simple words?

Is it possible that something that small is able to affect a life in *that* profound of a way?

Think about it, let that one smolder in your subconscious for a while, like slow burning embers.

Now let's talk about the next part of this proverb the, "is like apples of gold" part.

I think we can all agree that "is like" means "same as" or "equal to" - that's an easy one.

But then we get to apple. I know, I know you are probably going to tell me apple is a simple one, too - an apple is an apple, right?

But is it? Is it really?

I've been thinking about this one a lot.

In this context, apple isn't an apple like one that grows on the apple tree in your back yard. This apple is different, it's fruit.

And what do we know about fruit?

Well, first of all it's everywhere in the bible; "be fruitful and multiply", Cain brought fruits of the soil, then there is "fruit of the Spirit", and "go and bear fruit - fruit that will last".

Secondly, fruit doesn't necessarily mean fruit - it means *harvest,* abundance - the product. The product of where and how someone, (you) have spent time toiling, (thinking, talking, doing).

It's where you have spent your *precious* time.

The where, how, who and what you have invested in. You know exactly what I mean, the investment that is meant to be *your purpose here on earth* - that fruit.

So, what kind of purpose are you creating?

What kind of fruit are you bearing?

There is <u>always</u> fruit you know - good, bad and ugly.

And lastly, fruit is global - a *broad* term, hence; harvest, abundance.

In this way it is used for teaching when "the big picture" of the lesson is being illustrated. A specific fruit "apple, grapes" is used when the author/teacher wants a specific image to be brought to your mind and a very clear picture is needed to get the point across to you so there will be no doubt, no confusion.

Why is this important?

What difference does it make? Why apple?

I don't know.

Maybe it's because apples are a perfect size - not too small like grapes, (you'd have to carry a lot of them around to equal the size of an apple), or not too big like a gourd.

It could be because it fits in your hand perfectly - it's a handful.

Then again, maybe it's because apples are very important fruit for our health, for life.

"An apple a day keeps the doctor away", right?

I don't know - how about them apples, ha-ha-ha.

Does it matter why the proverb says apples? The answer is, "No not really".

The important thing is that you now have a very clear image in your mind of apples.

And that image has been planted and stamped there so when God tells you he has a Proverb 25:11 for you to do, that image of an apple will light up your brain like a Christmas tree.

Or the answer is yes - it's important because apple was used and not fruit so there must be a reason why this was done. But it is God's reason not ours.

Will we find out why?

Will the answer be revealed to us?

One day while we are praying and spending time with God or reading the bible will God light up our brain and explain it to us?

I don't know. Maybe.

What I do know is discussing this *is important* and has had made us think.

We haven't been able just to skip over this part like it's a no-brainer, like every word is not important.

Guess what - every word is extremely important, every word in the bible is extremely important and used specifically for purposes of revelation and education *and inspiration*.

So, we must pay attention - *all the time.*

Next important word... gold.

Now there is no mistaking gold. Gold is precious, gold is expensive and gold has been used for money for thousands of years. It represents *wealth* - great wealth.

In fact, I wish I had a couple of apples of gold right now. I definitely could wipe out all my bills, have some left over for some fun and then have some leftovers for a rainy day.

Do we all agree that the phrase - *is like apples of gold* must mean something important and valuable, something of great value and worth - something the average person would want and need and desire?

Good.

Do we agree that these apples of gold would make life easier, less difficult - make a major difference in someone's life - maybe even make such a difference that, that life would be forever changed?

Good.

Sounding even more important to you now?

Is it beginning to filter down to your toes why the author used this metaphor?

Apples of gold would mean prosperity, great wealth or abundance of any and all kinds for whoever has possession of them - *to give or to receive,* (giver or receiver).

Hmmm, again bringing the responsibility of the bearer back to you...

Because it's not enough that they are apples of gold; the importance is *these apples* of gold must get into the right hands for the full purpose which *only God knows.* This is where *these apples* take on a whole new meaning - an even greater meaning than before.

Now can you see when God gives you the assignment to deliver a message it isn't just some words - it isn't just any old message, it is a life-changing message - a life changer!

Something else about gold - it is "solid" and it has weight to it.

Sounds like the author really wanted to get our attention by using some powerful words - words with vivid and significant descriptions to get our attention.

Did it work?

Are you beginning to want more - more apples?

Okay, so what is the expectation of you delivering this package?

The expectation for God is that you will do it not only because he's asks you to do it, not only because the person you are delivering the package to needs it but because it's so chockfull of stuff that *it will change you and your life, too.*

It's a life-changer for you, too!

Wow, can it get any more important?

Actually, yes it can because this proverb doesn't just stop there. No way, it continues on with even more descriptions of urgency and importance.

Work to do: Journal for the next 2 days.

Day #1

Day #2

_____

_____

_____

_____

_____

_____

_____

_____

_____

_____

_____

_____

_____

_____

_____

_____

What is your interpretation of your last two days – any changes?

In your words? Intentions? Attitude?

Any missed opportunities?

_____

_____

_____

_____

_____

_____

_____

_____

_____

_____

_____

_____

_____

Chapter Four

...In Settings Of Silver

Really, wasn't "apples of gold" enough?

Shouldn't it be enough to get our attention?

Evidently the author did not think so. Evidently this proverb is *so important* that precious metal upon precious metal description was used to make sure the reader (you), would grasp the severity of this message that God has asked you (the reader), to deliver.

So, let's pick the important words in this last section apart – settings and silver.

Let's first tackle - settings.

Most of us have probably heard his word used in reference to the setting of a scene or play or an event and (especially for us women), the setting of a diamond or other jeweled ring. In either of these contexts it applies to "where" something is or where something is happening.

But let's examine these settings further.

Do you think that the author added these settings (of silver), to make it sound more decadent?

Or maybe the thought was, "I want to make sure whoever reads this realizes how smart and knowledgeable I am about precious metals?"

I seriously doubt it.

The longer you study the bible (especially Proverbs), you understand there is always a deeper meaning to the content and quite often more than *one* meaning.

Which is precisely *why it was written that way.* So, it can speak to *anyone and pertain to their particular situation at that time* - not an easy thing to do, by the way!

Back to "settings."

Yes, of course it refers to describing that not only were there apples of gold but that they were set in something made of silver. But hold on - there's something more.

It's about *where they were placed, how they were placed and naturally – who they* were placed there for.

Again, a reference back to how important it is to be careful where and how this message is delivered. It's about *timing.*

What happens if you open the oven door before the souffle' is ready?

Yup, you got it – deflated and sunken souffle'.

No one wants to eat it - it's undesirable and the person who it was made for is disappointed and angry and still hungry.

Timing is crucial - timing is not just the time of day or the day of the week or the month of the year. Timing is the place, under what circumstance and the intent in which the package is delivered - *your intent.*

Timing - if you are late, you miss it. If you are early, you miss it. If you don't show up at all - *you really have missed it!*

Then there's intent. Why is your intent so important?

Because the person you are delivering the message to will interpret *your intent* (motive and attitude), and that my friend - will influence their acceptant or not.

Ah-hah!

Again, *see how important you the messenger are.*

Think about all the times in *your* life when someone has given you an important piece of advice or shared a vital piece of information that changed the course of a decision you needed to make or affected something you were going to do - or even made the difference in a relationship that you were about to get into or not get into.

Wasn't the messenger just as important as the message? Don't say "no" because you're not being honest.

Of course, the deliverer of the information was important.

You had to trust them, right?

Why else would you listen or take their advice or believe what they were telling you was true?

And "how" they were telling you the information was just as important, right?

If they were open, honest and concerned for you - you knew they had your best interests at heart. They were telling you something to help you and not to harm you.

But if they were unconcerned, disinterested or saying it sarcastically or in a "shifty" way - you ran from the message or maybe you didn't but you should have.

And you thought this was a simple, straight-forward proverb.

Think again.

And truly, that is what these proverbs are supposed to do – to make you think.

Next - silver.

When this proverb was written, silver was the next best precious medal and if you couldn't have gold you wanted silver. It is shiny and catches your eye quickly.

Hmmm... catches your eye quickly, this could be a good reason why the author used it here -to accentuate the importance of; the setting, the timing, the motive and attitude.

The - who, what, where and when of the mission that God has given you to do.

And why do you think this is all so important?

Why God inspired the author to write this proverb for all of us - for all the people over the last thousand plus years who has read this proverb. Why?

Are you ready for this?

He did it so all of us can live an abundant life.

So, we can live a life of abundance - aligned with him, aligned with his spirit.

He did it so our spirit and his are intertwined and forever one.

So, you can live a life of abundance - rich in all things.

And by the way - we aren't talking, or just talking, about money here - abundance does not just refer to money or wealth. I mean, it could be money or possessions but it means so much more - love, respect, peace, joy, family, relationships, intelligence, forgiveness, opportunities -

And the list goes on and on and on...

The more we listen, the more we learn, the more we obey *(not in a negative way)*, but by taking what we have heard and learned and then putting it into action for the maximum positive affect in our lives and in our world.

I'll say it again, the message you carry - the package you deliver is not just for the recipient, it's for you.

Why?

Because you are the recipient too!

You're the recipient of the blessing that comes from your obedience - of accepting the challenge, that *mission impossible.*

You are 007, a secret agent - *a secret agent for God.*

"Goldfinger" - sorry I couldn't resist that one!

Chapter Five

Bees and B's...First Let Me Tell You About The Bees

"Hey, why are you spending time talking about bees when most people try to avoid them, at all costs?"

Bees are annoying, they sting and if you are allergic to that bee sting - "LOOK OUT!"

Because, for you to deliver the package in the manner it truly is intended you must be like a bee and to be like a bee you must have some respect for that bee you are supposed to be like.

So, it's my job to throw some "bee" knowledge your way and for you to catch it, catch on and catch up to what is going on.

Now bees don't come knocking on your door and say, "Here I am at your service" as their way of *earning* your respect - a bee is a bee and we just need to have some respect for them.

We need to respect them because they were made by God for

a purpose - a very important purpose. Just like us, just like God made *us* for a very important purpose.

What exactly are bees?
What do bees do?
What happens if they don't?
Why do they do it?
How do they know to do it?

Wikipedia tells us they are flying insects that produce honey and beeswax and are found everywhere, except Antarctica. They feed on nectar and pollen from flowers and flowering plants = pollination.

A vital thing for us humans if we want to continue to enjoy beauty in nature.

Did you know there are over 20,000 species of bees?

Well, you do now and did you know they are the most efficient pollinating insect we have?

If not, you know it now.

They swarm - which you've probably seen before and many species live in colonies. Again, something you may have seen. They are part of the food chain - food for birds and they communicate with each other, (read about the wiggle dance).

Many of the colonized species have a queen and to make the colony productive they have a highly efficient division of labor - bees coming and going dawn to dusk.

Busy as a bee, right? I know you've heard of that one. Sounds like bees are a little OCD, what do you think?

Again, why are we talking about bees?

Well, if you haven't figured it out yet, I will tell you.

Since bees are the most efficient insect for pollinating and pollination is so extremely important that we need to be just like bees - then we should get some pointers on how and why they are so efficient so we can be that efficient, too.

Right? We need to be for delivering the package, (that message God has asked us to pollinate someone with).

That's right, I said it - pollinate.

Us taking the message from God, delivering it to its destination so the package can be opened and produce "honey" - *the miracle God intended all along.*

Is it such a hard stretch to think that we are like bees and need to act more like them?

I don't think so. In fact, we have a lot in common with them.

Bees fly. We walk, run and jog - all modes of transportation.

Bees sting. We hurt those who have hurt us, (verbally or physically).

Bees pollinate. We work.

From pollination bees produce honey and beeswax. From our work we produce money, art, literature and music - *and* we care for others, all of which are vital to our species.

Bees live in colonies. We live in colonies, too - at least most of us. Exceptions are hermits because even our homeless and those living on the streets are part of some type of community.

Bees are the most efficient at pollination and we, well we must be the most efficient at something- even if that *something* is being human.

Bees swarm.

We swarm - just see what happens after someone throws the first punch at a baseball, football or basketball ball game, a swarm of crazed fans and athletes at a feeding frenzy.

Bees are part of the food chain.

Since humans are pretty far up on the food chain this one is a little difficult but here goes; we eventually decompose and part of what's left moves on by some mode of transportation to be re-invented into something or someone else.

How about that one?

Bees communicate. We do to - not always well, but we do it.

Bees are found everywhere except Antarctica, sounds like us.

And lastly, bees have a queen. We have God: faith, trust, belief, obedience, joy, grace, forgiveness and love.

Oh, and *many of us* <u>are</u> OCD.

And let's not forgot - bees are determined little critters. They attack that flower and they'll attack you, *too* if you get in their way.

They are tenacious, goal-oriented and persistent - and they doggedly, day after day do their job.

Now you may say - that's their instinct to do that, they are instinctual insects.

Maybe, but guess what?

So are we - instinctual, I mean.

Don't we have a built-in mechanism which strongly urges us *to* mate and procreate?

Don't we seek love and validation and go to great lengths to get them?

Yes, we do.

And no - it's not just our "hormones".

Yes, the procreation part is driven by hormones but the love and validation - hey man, there's a different driver driving that bus.

Even after the hormones are long gone we continue to long for love, companionship and validation. That's our instinct embedded in our DNA by our Creator - *for our Creator.*

Yes, we give and receive love, companionship and validation with others of our species but, the truth is - the "longing" was always intended for our Creator, the Source of who we are and *why* we are.

When you are in the flow with God, when you are in the current of the river - don't you feel connected with God?

But when you are fighting the river, struggling against the current - you feel alone, abandoned and hopeless, right?

What do you think that is all about?

Some red-headed chick down the street or some dark, mysterious stranger you've had your little eyes on?

No.

That hole in your heart can only be filled by God who created you, the one who unconditionally loved you before you existed and continues to love you unconditionally - no matter what you do.

Him - your Source, my Source - everyone's Source.

Okay, back to bees.

Seems we are already a lot like bees except for that super - efficiency one.

A-hah!

Sounds like the one we need to work on.

Possibility that queen one, too - and you know, both those things are what this book and this proverb are all about.

What happens if you leave the yeast out of your homemade bread recipe?

The answer is you get a brick that will mold - worthless and soon to be green and stinky.

Why did I aptly place this tidbit here?

To get your attention silly, just in case you're starting to nod off.

Seriously, it's here to remind us one more time how important delivering that message is, (adding the yeast) and not leaving the perfect "how, what, when, where and who" out.

Then again, maybe just a little bit it's here to *wake you up.*

What have we learned and what will it mean if we act like these little critters?

I hope we've gathered some respect for bees and come to realize even insects are important in what they do and what they can teach us. Just look at all the different species of animals, birds, fish, reptiles and insects and trees, plants and flowers that God created.

Think of all the thought that went into each one, all so different - all dependent, independent and inter-dependent of each other.

Now the B's...

Be giving - to yourself and others
Be generous - again, to yourself and others
Be quiet - and listen, quit talking and thinking so much
    Be bold - and courageous, step out in faith
Be trusting – in yourself and others
Be a doer- don't just talk about it - do it!
Be sensitive -- look beneath the surface, put yourself in their shoes and understand
    Be kind - to yourself and others
Be encouraging - to everyone, including yourself - be a Barnabas
    Be first to - forgive, always

Be love - loving to others, (not just your dog)
　　Be open - and honest
Be positive - beware of blessing-stealers, anything that wants to steal your joy
　　Be blessed - and be a blessing
Be humble - don't boast, remember if appropriate - God will boast about you
　　Be victorious - be obedient, that is the first step
Be wondrous - and in awe of everything you see
　　Be a yes man - for God
Be a person who feels - and let your emotions be your emotional gauge
　　Be sensitive to others - always, it's the second step
Be honest - it always comes back to you
　　Be wise - in all situations, it's the third step.

And lastly, be listening for that small still voice, (God's voice) over all the loud noise in your life - your job, your kids, your spouse, your friends and your negative emotions.

Think, "Is this the way you are?" If not - why not? Mark 10:17 - what do you value?

It's not just money we are talking about, here.

It's anything in your life that you give value to, spend time with, desire and want more of. You must be willing to surrender it - surrender all, continuously.

That's right, I said it - continuously.

It's not a one-time shot and then, "Forget about it".

Surrendering is a daily thing and will be different each day depending where your heart and mind are at that time.

That's why it's so hard to follow God all the time, every day - because, "we *all* are the rich man **in** the above scripture." Our riches are just different, but *each and every one of us, is that man.*

So, what do you really value?

And can you surrender it to God not knowing whether it **will** come back to you.

Your assignment: Read the "B's" again and for the next 2 days put as many of them into practice as you can.

Day #1
Journal what happened

_____

_____

_____

_____

_____

_____

_____

_____

_____

_____

_____

_____

_____

Day #2 – Journal what happened.

_____

_____

_____

_____

_____

_____

_____

_____

_____

_____

_____

_____

_____

_____

_____

_____

Did you discover personal limitations to doing any of them or negative patterns to overcome?

_____

_____

_____

_____

_____

_____

_____

_____

_____

_____

_____

_____

_____

_____

Who or what is influencing you?

_____

_____

_____

_____

_____

_____

_____

_____

_____

_____

_____

_____

_____

_____

_____

Set several goals for yourself for the next week:

Chapter Six

How About The Queen?

The one in charge of the hive, the one the bees protect at all costs.

Well for us, God is in charge of our life, (if we let him) and *he* does the protecting. Lucky for us.

His "hive" isn't physically down here on earth with all us little worker bees but his omnipotence allows him to see what's happening and know what we need. And it is his job to be working out the details even when *we* don't know what's going on.

Clever, huh?

Well it is and a good thing for us. But he does need something in return.

Why?

Because that's how a relationship works. That's how a two-way, reciprocal relationship is supposed to work - back and forth, give and take.

What he needs from us little busy bees down here is to pollinate - pollinate the world, by spreading the word, by delivering the package.

Why do you think King David was a man after God's own heart?

Consistent faith - it bridged the gap.

David's unwavering faith in God sustained him in between the high and lows of his life - his successes and failures, his obedience and his disobedience.

God never failed him.

David experienced some consequences from his disobedience but that's just the natural order of life.

We kick a marble topped table with all our might - we're gonna break a toe, (or two).

We're talking on our cell phone while we are driving and the car in front of us stops abruptly - there's going to be an accident, cause and effect.

Just like David and just like our bees we need to live our life fully invested - fully invested in our God and in the "assignment" he has given to us.

We should do this because it is important - it's so important that we should never let anything get in the way of doing it, nothing.

You see, David pollinated.

God told him what to do - he did it.

When he remembered to seek and ask God - good things happened, victory.

When he forgot to ask God what to do or did something without putting God first (ie Bathsheba), failure and then - the fallout from it.

I want to be like David but without the bad decisions. It's a tall order - but one we all need to strive for.

So, let's delve a little deeper into the word pollinate and what it means in the year 2022.

Pollination has to happen for fertilization to happen and fertilization brings about fruitfulness, enrichment and growth.

Have to sow if we want a harvest - if we want to reap.

Good pollination, good sowing = good harvest.

So, what's good pollination?

Good pollination is the right pollen transferred to the right flower, an example of this would be; daisy to daisy, but not daisy to tree.

That won't work, see the difference?

So again, we are being brought back to the cornerstone of this proverb - the right stuff (message), being delivered to the right person. And let's not forget - the right place and the right time.

The truth is, we are pollinating all the time - every day.

That's the good news.

The bad news is - it's not always the right pollen to the right flower.

Quite often it's the wrong pollen to any flower, plant, animal or mineral - anything that will stand still for a second and anything that can hear.

It doesn't even need to be able to hear, we'll still try to pollinate it. In fact, we'll even talk to the dog or to our self if we have no one else to talk to. It's a good thing David didn't have facebook, twitter and tweet back then - lucky for him. Just think if he did. His escapade with Bathsheba would have been chirped and warbled across the kingdom almost before it was done happening...

This above truth is why there is so much confusion, negativity and drama in your life and in the world - bad pollination.

Bad pollination is globally devastating in the year 2022 as compared to let's say David's time.

So, my little *chick-a-dees,* watch what pollen you are spreading and don't forget about the pollen someone is trying to fertilize you with. That gossip you are listening to even though you know you shouldn't.

And there's the confidences that pop out of your mouth that you promised to keep - that ruin the harvest and ruin lives.

Remember - *kick the marble-top table, you're gonna be in pain and limping.*

Do you know why God created bees?

It was not just for pollinating you know. And why do you think he also created all those billions of ants scurrying around everywhere? It wasn't to spray insecticide on, swat at or step on.

No siree-bob, they were designed as examples to teach us and to motivate us to realize that the packages we are delivering can; create beauty, move mountains and change the world - *or not.*

And that "not" may mean a halt in the progress or even destruction of what God has carefully and painstakingly already built.

So - pay attention and live with intention.

Don't follow the crowd and be like sheep following each other into the slaughter house. Stay tuned-in to your Source, your Creator because he already knows what's around the corner and down the street for you. Not like you - who can only see until the road curves.

Everyday God gives you opportunities to improve your life and improve the lives of others.

What are you doing with those opportunities?

Do you even see them?

Or are you so mesmerized by your phone, TV, the internet and facebook - your eyes glued to the screen and getting carpal tunnel from the mouse. And because you are so mesmerized that your life has passed you by - "I mean your *real* life".

Wake up! Look up!

And look around you - life is meant to be abundant.

I know we have said that before but I don't think you have fully absorbed this fantastic concept. Life is amazing, exciting, filled with awe and wonder, beauty, joy and buckets of blessings.

The catch is - you have to be looking.

They are not going to walk up to you, poke you in the chest or slap you in the face and say, *"I'm here - take advantage of me".*

You have to be able to see them, be sensitive to the spirit - to that still, small voice, so you can recognize your blessings.

Cause on a daily basis God is going to bring them into your life. Just like an assembly line with a big, old conveyor belt moving from the day you are born to the day your flesh body wrinkles up and dies and your spirit floats to its next destination.

And I know a little about conveyor belts.

i grew up in Youngstown just a few miles away from Lordstown, Ohio and one of the biggest car factories in the United States until the Recession of 1978. Also, the day that caught Youngstown - Steel Valley with its' pants down, great example of "walking around with your eyes shut but pretending to see".

"Zombies in Slumberland" would have been a great title for that movie - tens of thousands of people brutally awakened from their dreams in one day, the "American Dream" – gone.

What am I saying?

I'm saying don't separate yourself from the opportunities because they are your blessings - and *your* blessings are blessings God has not just hand-picked for you but ones - <u>so you can help others.</u>

The package, remember?

We are talking about delivering the package and not just the package like there is only one that God will ask you to deliver in your lifetime. That conveyor belt that's delivering blessings to you is also bringing packages for you to deliver to others.

You want blessings every day, right? Well, guess what - so does everybody else.

Hello, are you listening? Do you get it?

Can you see it in your mind - in your life?

Do it because it's important to you to do it - not because you think you are supposed to fix someone else.

God does the fixing - not you. Just deliver the package at the right time, in the right place, to the right person with the right attitude.

That's your job - let God do the rest and you move on to the next thing. Go back to the conveyor belt pick up your next assignment and be grateful about it, *be very grateful.*

That is the key to pollination.

Be grateful you are alive, be grateful you have another day to enjoy your blessing and to bless someone else, be grateful that God has chosen *you* to deliver packages.

Otherwise, "What is the point of you being here"?

Just to accumulate possessions?

Really, did you think that's why God took the time to create you -- so you can just sit around on your stuff?

Think again my friend.

Did you see the movie "Bee Movie" with Jerry Seinfeld as the voice of the main bee character?

Yes?

Good, if no - then go rent it and watch it.

It's a great movie and brings home the point of what would happen if there were no bees to pollinate - or more precisely what happened when the bees went on strike and decided to stop pollinating.

Of course, disaster happened.

And in a world where there were no flowers and all the plant-life was disappearing it took a miracle and several heroes to save the day and jump-start pollination and get it humming along again.

Sound like a "kid movie"?

Wrong, it definitely was not designed for kids.

It was written to get the attention of adults and not just about the obvious crisis of bee extinction. This movie is a spiritual creation and it's a perfect fit for what we are talking about in this Proverb.

What would happen if bees stopped doing their job?

What would happen if no one followed God and stopped carrying the message?

What would happen if packages stopped being delivered?

What would happen?

Extinction.

Extinction of life as we have known up to this point, that's what.

People would be totally selfish and self-absorbed.

No one would help anyone when a crisis or natural disaster happened or when children were starving. There would be no hero's or acts of kindness, no pay it forward, no "thank-you's" or compliments - this planet would be a very dark place to live and living here would be not just be depressing, but treacherous.

If someone wanted what you had they would just take it. Without morals, without ethics without a belief in something larger than us - we are left alone with our *very human nature* - nomads.

Pretty power stuff, huh?

Without pollination - everything eventually withers and dies. And while all of this is happening life feels empty - life feels meaningless, because it is.

Without pollinating - without us delivering the "good news" to others so our Source, the Source of Life can change the course of people's lives - miracles don't happen.

That means in your life, too!

Remember the analogy of the rock in the pond - the ripple effect goes all the way to the shore, it affects everything in that pond, right?

Same with us - cause and effect.

It's true whether you choose to believe it or not. Just try to do or say something without there being an effect or consequence from it.

Look around, pay attention - recognize what's really happening every day in your life and in the lives of others.

So, get in the flow - get in the river, the river of life.

Physical life here on earth is not tangible - it is temporary.

Life is spiritual.

Everything you say and do, everyone that surrounds you and everything that the future holds - it's all spiritual and falls under the law of spirit.

And, the only way for us to navigate this spiritual journey of ours through its narrow locks and channels is to have a road map that sets our course.

Guess what?

We do - it's called the bible. And not only does it navigate us, it is our instructions for building an abundant life - a perfect life, the perfect here and now *and future.*

You want the proof?

Andy Griffith.

The Andy Griffith Show. He's the proof - Sheriff Andy Taylor and, Aunt Bee, Opie, Barney and so on and so on...

Every episode a gold mine, a treasure trove of the bible in action; trials and crisis's, opportunities to choose right or wrong, blessings or consequences - all wrapped up neatly at the end with a big red bow.

And how about the book and subsequently the movie, "Scrooged" - with its 3 ghosts - past, present and future.

It is also a great example of what we're talking about here.

And my favorite, "It's a Wonderful Life".

Parallel lives, the one we're living and the one that *could be* if we were never born

Or maybe the one that *could have been* if we had done something different.

Today I read something that made me sad, then happy and then cry all the in the span of fifteen minutes. It was a story about a teacher and a little boy.

It went something like this...

Mrs. Smith had just got hired to teach 5th grade. It was her first job as a teacher and she was very excited.

She had vowed that she would treat every child the same and never play favorites.

On her first day she walked into her class room and saw thirty little faces and just knew she would make a difference in all their lives.

But, there was just one problem twenty-nine of them were interested in what she said and eager to learn. But one - was not.

Twenty-nine of them came to school every day ready, their homework done with clean faces, hair and clothes. One did not, his name was Bobby.

Mrs. Smith slowly found herself becoming critical of Bobby and when the other children made fun of him for not having his homework or for his disheveled appearance – she did nothing to stop them.

And every day she became more and more irritated with Bobby.

Her husband noticed that when he asked her how her day had been, instead of sharing positive stories all she now was sharing were negative ones about this boy who was "trouble". Bobby.

Day after day it was the same.

And every day she liked being a teacher less and less.

One day her husband got so tired of hearing what Bobby had done, that he blurted out, "Did you ever think there might be a reason why this boy is like this?"

Sadly, she had not. But didn't want him to think she wasn't a good teacher So she said, "He's always been trouble", and walked away.

But when she was alone she couldn't stop thinking, "What if I'm wrong?"

The next day she looked back at the evaluations the teachers before her had given Bobby.

His 1st grade teacher said he was "out-going, curious and friendly".

His 2nd grade teacher said he was a "bright boy with much promise" but sad at times because his mother was ill.

His 3rd grade teacher said he had become quieter since his mother's death and hoped it would not have long-term effects on him.

And his 4th grade teacher had labeled him "withdrawn and dull-witted" spending most of the day staring out the window.

She put down the evaluations and with tears in her eyes she asked God to forgive her and to help her love Bobby.

From that day on she began to encourage Bobby, adding a warm smile and a touch whenever she could.

At Christmas all the students brought her brightly-colored gifts wrapped neatly with matching ribbons except Bobby - his was lumpy from the brown paper grocery bag and twine.

But she didn't care, when she opened his she exclaimed in joy when she saw the rhinestone bracelet with several stones missing and the bottle of perfume with only a small amount left inside because she knew in her heart where they had come from.

She put on the bracelet and sprayed on the perfume like it was the most-expensive one that any store had to offer. And at the end of the day after all the children had left except Bobby, he whispered to her as he walked out the door, "You smell just like my mom on Christmas Day", and he smiled.

Seven years went by and Mrs. Smith received a note from Bobby on graduation day, he wrote, "Thank you for encouraging me. You are the best teacher I've ever had".

He signed it Bobby Stone.

Four more years went by and she received another note from Bobby on his graduation day from college. It read, "Thank you, for all your encouragement. You still are the best teacher I've ever had." and signed it.

Bobby Stone.

The years flew by and one day Mrs. Smith received a note from Bobby, he wrote, "I'm getting married and since my father died two years ago would you please come and be my family at the wedding?

By the way, you're still the best teacher I ever had. This time it wasn't signed Bobby. This time the name was a little longer.

Bobby Stone MD.

On the day of the wedding Mrs. Smith was proud to share in Bobby's joy and after the ceremony he hugged her and thanked her for making a difference in his life. Without her he never would have become a doctor and have the courage to marry the woman of his dreams.

Mrs. Smith smiled, drew him close and whispered, "Without you I never would have known how to be a teacher".

Hmm...think about that one for a while.

My friend, "Be ready".

God is going to send a package your way - a blessing, a solution, a conviction. So, be ready to catch it before it speeds past you.

And really - that's exactly how I imagine it is.

God, like the wind, blows the answer your way and you have to be standing there with a big catcher's mitt poised to catch it before it turns into a foul ball or an error and you miss it entirely.

Can you see it?

Can you imagine it?

Close your eyes and visualize. Do it until it becomes real to you, until it is part of you then you will be ready. Then *you* won't miss *your* blessing!

Because, if you aren't ready and if you neglect pollination, it might just find someone who **is** ready to catch it.

And then, poof! You missed your blessing. Or worse still, the package recipient misses their blessing.

Either way because of *you* - blessings are missed!

Pollinate!

So, what is this miracle we've alluded to?

Your assignment: Close your eyes for 60 seconds and imagine yourself as a bee. Can you see you? Good!

Then journal for the next two days seeing yourself as a bee and journal how you have pollinated.

Day #1

_____

_____

_____

_____

_____

_____

_____

_____

_____

_____

_____

_____

_____

Susan Farah

Day #2

_____

_____

_____

_____

_____

_____

_____

_____

_____

_____

_____

_____

_____

_____

_____

_____

Do you have a Bobby Stone in your life?

Think back and really think, were you the clueless teacher or were you the enlightened one?

_____

_____

_____

_____

_____

_____

_____

_____

_____

_____

_____

_____

_____

Chapter Seven

There Isn't Just One, You Know, Miracles That Is

There are millions happening every day, all over the world. They happen in big cities, small villages, during the day, in the middle of the night, to the old, the young and the unborn. They happen in the rain, in the snow and in the moonlight, they happen while people are awake or asleep, while they are smiling or screaming out in terror - and they happen whether anyone knows it or not.

So, *"What is a miracle"?*

That is part of the problem right there - understanding what a miracle is.

Most people think that a miracle is a supernatural thing - that it can only be a supernatural thing, like being cured instantaneously from cancer or being brought back after your heart has stopped for ten minutes.

Yes of course, those are miracles. But those are only the

miracles that get advertised, shouted from the roof-tops - the big ones.

Waking up every morning having another day to celebrate life - is a miracle. A baby being born perfect - with no defect or blemish, that's a miracle.

Paying all your bills and having money left over to take your family out to dinner and a movie or take them to Disney World - that's a miracle.

Graduating college and becoming a teacher, a nurse or a doctor - that's a miracle.

Being loved and respected by everyone you know and everyone you meet - that's a miracle.

You know what else is a miracle?

Being encouraged, being lifted-up, your soul nourished or your body fed by a stranger.

Smiling, after you've been caught in the rain and you're wet and cold after you had to change a flat tire - that's a miracle, too.

Why?

Because the odds are against it, that's why.

Holding the door open for the person behind you, paying the cashier an extra five dollars and saying, "Use it for the next person paying their bill" - that's a miracle.

Not getting caught up in the office gossip or office negativity.

Allowing someone to get the parking space you have waited for - that's a miracle.

All these are simple miracles that can happen every day - if we so chose.

That's the rub, we have to choose…

Free will, remember?

It's too bad we have that.

Let's be honest, you've thought about that one before, I know you have. And just maybe God's thought about that one, too. Life sure would be easier if God could go around zapping people all day - making them do the right thing. Wouldn't it?

Hey, I would love to have that power - we all would.

Close your eyes for a minute and imagine you could blink or send a lightning bolt to force people to do good – not hurt or destroy others.

But sadly, God did give us free will and that's why we have miracles.

Or more precisely - that is why miracles *need to happen.*

And that's why God needs us. Otherwise he wouldn't really need us. He loves us and wants a relationship with us - but he wouldn't *need* us.

Think long and hard about that one for a minute.

The other thing to think about is - we *need* to make miracles happen.

You need to make miracles happen!

Yes, you do, we all do. Otherwise we really would be totally selfish, self-centered and obnoxious individuals. It *would* really all be about us - all the time.

Yuck!

Think about the most conceded, selfish person you know- egotistical to the max.

What if everyone was like that, OMG!

"What a nightmare!" Our own human nature - run amuck...

God in his mercy knew without guidance and a purpose, a true purpose - humans would have a hard time not messing things up.

Hence, the job of delivering packages, of being messengers - human angels on earth, fulfilling our "need to be needed".

And not needed just by a loved one - but by a stranger.

That's the crucial component - strangers. Where there are no obligations. And the miracle for us is - we get the miracle at the same time, saving ourselves from being narcissistic and arrogant jerks.

So, just do it for the purpose of it, for the obedience of it - for the love of it and because that's God's assignment for you. And in doing that, you've done it for the right reason - it's the right thing to do.

I watched a movie about Beatrix Potter the other day.

In fact, I watched it twice. Both times I was filled with wonder and amazement.

What a package she delivered!

Oops, there were actually two; the creation of beautiful characters and books that changed the lives of hundreds of thousands of children. And for an encore, the donation of hundreds of acres of private land to her country for preservation.

There were other packages she delivered too, you know; her boldness to go out and market herself in a time and place where that was not the norm - a trailblazer for others.

Not marrying for money as so many countless women did again in that time and place - trailblazing again, but standing up for the man she did want to marry against the pressure of her parents. And when his untimely death took him, she did not lose her mind or lose herself in a marriage of convenience - but boldly forged ahead and delivered that big second package, and finding her second love in the process.

Think of all the children whose lives would have sadly empty of those stories.

And think of her fellow countrymen missing out on that beautiful gift of nature she left behind - *if, she hadn't delivered those packages.*

So, what are we saying here?

Are we saying that delivering a package is following through on a creation placed in our imagination, standing up for what is right even though we may be afraid or being courageous in our godly convictions?

Are we saying that these packages don't have to have a single address or a single name attached to them, to be delivered to?

Yes, that's exactly what I am saying.

Ah-hah, bet that opens up your mind and gets you thinking!

Where do you think your godly convictions come from or the ability to imagine something new, beautiful or exciting and then turn it into reality?

Did you think that was just you?

Please, it's not that simple.

All those things are miracles - inspired by God to you to be delivered to the *world* in some fashion to fulfill his miracles here on earth so, in turn, others can pay it forward.

And all this delivering and paying forward is the end-product of God's love-- solely for the purpose of spreading His love to the world.

I think some of you may have heard this before.

You know, the "great commission".

Did ya think telling someone about Jesus is all the "great commission" is about?

If that is you - you've missed half the message, at least up to this point.

Maybe you have been telling others about Jesus but now it's time to finish the other half of the assignment - *to do what he did and not just talk about what he did.*

Can I say that one again, **"Do what he did and not just talk about what he did."**

It's time to show the world *what you can do, what they can do* - not just what *Jesus* did and can *do* for *them*.

Powerful stuff, huh...

Bet you didn't realize how much was jam-packed into this one little proverb, did you?

One last little thing about Beatrix.

"Her characters were real to her - she saw them, talked to them and they talked back to her and were as real as any actual person or animal to her. She treated them with respect and took care of them just as if they were real animals in need of food, shelter and love".

She validated them, she validated their existence - they were important to her and to the world.

Beatrix understood this proverb; that to truly deliver, *"a ward aptly placed is like apples of gold in settings of silver"*, it must be so important to the messenger that it be delivered that they will go to any lengths to make it happen.

See it through no matter what even if it means being labeled eccentric or any of the other labels I'm sure people tried to stick on her.

That's the phenomenon and that's what makes it phenomenal.

Every day, 365 days a year - you have the opportunity at work, at home and with your friends to perform a miracle that will change the world.

Don't you want to change the world - maybe even a little bit?

Are you skeptical?

Think that maybe you might be able to affect someone a little bit but - change the world, *never.*

Wrong - *you are so wrong.*

Again, the rock in the pond - it ripples all the way to the shore, remember?

And that is just what we see at the surface and anyone who has studied icebergs knows: only the tip is visible above water - the biggest part of it is underneath, under the surface, out of sight.

And so is the affect that rock has on that pond.

And so is the affect you have on the world.

Yes, you might be able to see a change in someone or something. But what you don't see is the most important part, what is happening beneath the surface, beneath their skin.

That's where the stuff is truly happening.

That's what affects them and affects the ones around them. Which in turn affects the ones around them and so on and so on - until it makes its' way around the world.

Do we have to march seven times around something and shout the walls of Jericho down or are you willing to believe this truth?

Will you choose to fully embrace the complexity and the completeness of this proverb - this challenge to you and for you?

Take down the *"Do not disturb"* sign that has been hanging around your neck or tattooed to your forehead and come alive!

Join the group of those who are *living their life* and not just watching their life pass by like a parade *and* pass them by without the "abundant life" actually happening to them.

Don't be one of them. There are too many of them already.

Be passionate about God's challenge to you. Seriously devote your passion to it. Never give up even if something interferes with you delivering that package or message.

Keep trying.

And, if you delivered the message and suddenly there it is again, *"Deliver that package again to that person"*.

Do it again, because - what people hate today they will love tomorrow.

What?

Really, is that true?

Yup, most of the time, it's another one of those "phenomenon's".

You see some people need an idea or piece of advice to bounce around the inside of their brain like "pacman" for a while until someone comes along and delivers that same message to them again but maybe a little different this time – packaged and wrapped a little differently.

Then, WHAM-BAM - thank you ma'am" they love it. They've accepted it and it now does the miracle it was supposed to do.

Go figure - hate turns to love, a two-edged sword. True story...

I can think of things in my life that now I recognize were those miracles - people delivering that perfect "word" to me.

A doctor's name and phone number that changed my life from misery back to "normal".

Information about "her new job" from a neighbor which spurred me on to get the same training she did and ultimately giving me my career as a nurse, just to name two.

But I wonder, "What about the packages that people didn't deliver to me"?

What about those?"

What were they, when were they supposed to be delivered?

How would my life be different if they would have been delivered?

Would I be smarter, healthier, richer or happier?

Would I be living somewhere different or doing something else with my life?

Would it be a good thing or a bad thing?

And, what about the people who didn't follow through and deliver those messages to me? Their assignments from God?

How are their lives "less than" because they didn't deliver those packages?

What about the miracles they didn't get because they were too busy or afraid or unconcerned to play post office?

And consider those assignments that were too important for God to just let fall through the cracks, so he found someone else to deliver them. Someone who was ready and was waiting for the opportunity to do something incredulous - *and they did.*

Because remember, some people are excited about doing miracles.

They are energized and have been on the look-out, wearing binoculars just waiting and totally ready to jump in their "FedEx" truck and make that delivery.

If you neglect it, it will go find someone else to do it - it can be that powerful.

It has to be - it's coming from God and someone is going to get the blessing from the delivering.

It can be you - or not.

Your life can be more abundant - or not.

You choose · it's your choice.

You can't blame anyone else - you can try, but God knows *and* so do you.

Now, I have something provocative for you to think about.

I am only writing this book, (and others) as a result of a negative thing that happened to me and along with this negative thing there was the messenger who delivered it.

Out of that negative thing with its' messenger came a major life change, great satisfaction for me and life-affecting changes for others.

What about that?

What do we say about that? What's your answer for that?

God doesn't just use perfectly good people or perfectly good situations.

God uses what he knows will get the job done, period. This could be disturbing news.

"Hey, sorry to burst your bubble", but I bet there are just as many miracles coming from the negative packages and the negative deliverers as from the positive ones.

Judas, remember?

So just don't think the "good" people are special and get to be King or Queen "FedEx" for the day.

Everyone's special. God is not prejudiced, right?

Everyone one gets equal time, equal love and equal pruning; which is really lucky for all of us because God's crown has "unconditional" embroidered across it.

So, now back to me as an example...

Up until six years ago I had not written a book. In fact, I had never thought about writing a book, it was not in my wheelhouse. I had written short stories for college, newsletters and brochures for Second Chances, policies and procedures for several different jobs I had - but no books.

It never occurred to me that I could or should write a book.

Then this crazy, scary "stopped-dead-in-my-tracks" experience happened to me and one day I just sat down at the computer and started typing.

I don't remember if I had the logical thought to write what happened, or if I sat down at the computer and suddenly found myself writing down what happened.

All I know is there I was pouring out on paper what was in my head.

Now don't get me wrong it was important to get it out, I do know that.

But it wasn't urgent.

It wasn't a fervor-filled obsession. It was just important.

But the odd thing, it was more than just an explanation of what had happened. It showed up in book - form in my head, with scenes and conversations and even humor.

And it kept coming.

Almost every day at some point I would sit at the computer and start typing. Pretty quickly I found out that I needed to wait for the *"urge"* and the inspiration to do it.

If I didn't, what I did try to write was not good - not good at all. But the more I tuned in to the voice inside me, the spirit inside - the more it flowed.

I guess that's what being in the flow is all about. Like being in a river. I hope it never stops.

If you go with the flow of the river you get down stream, where you need and want to go. But if you fight against the stream - you're stuck in the same place for a long time. And you are tired, you've used up all your energy fighting and now you have nothing left for the important part *and* for the fun part - *the fruit of your labor.*

And guess what else?

Not only was all of this going on in my life but then, in my brain up pops a list of titles of the "books" (plural), that I was going to write and in ranking order.

Huh?

Sound a little crazy?

Well, no joke -- I thought it was a lot crazy. But it's true.

Yup, at the same time I was typing the technicolor movie projecting across the wideangle, screen in my head - I was getting "future assignments" of what to do.

But, not so much as to interfere with the job I was trying to do in keeping up with the thoughts in my head, and writing them down before they were lost. Just enough to make a good outline - the title of the book and a sentence or two of what it was going to be about. And in some cases, what the cover of the book was supposed to look like.

No joke.

It's true, the covers of *Matchmaker - the Perfect Match, Shells, So and E3 - The Barnabas Touch* - were pictures in my head.

The other thing I knew was important was that I was supposed to write down exactly what was showing up in my head even if it didn't make sense and then, wait for the interpretation - the rest of it to show up.

Now, many writers are probably saying, "Well, that is how it works for me, too". Well, maybe.

But, what I do know is that I didn't write these books.

I never have written a book.

I am just a secretary, typing up what the author is dictating which just happens to be lighting up my brain.

There, I said it.

"When you are the recipient of an all-important package *and* you accept that package:

– You have just jumped into the river.

> – You are now in the flow (with God), and what happens next - how your life unfolds is a direct result of that package deliverance and your acceptance."

And it's still happening.

But, there is no guarantee, no promise that riding this wave of flowing water will continue forever - especially if you take it for granted and don't work on staying atop it, (much like a surfer practicing to stay on that surf board).

So, what am I really saying?

There was this very old, wise man in this small village way up in the mountains of Peru, I think, and one day a lesser-wise man came up to him and asked, "Did you hear about little Juan, his rich uncle gave him a pony, isn't that wonderful?"

"We'll see", the very old, wise man replied.

A month later little Juan fell of the horse and broke his leg. The lesser-wise man came up to the very old, wise man and said, "Isn't it terrible about little Juan?"

"We'll see", said the very old, wise man.

A month later big Juan, little Juan's uncle gave Juan a $100 bill for being such a brave little boy. The lesser-wise man again searched out the very old, wise man and said, "Isn't that wonderful news about little Juan?"

And again, the very old, wise man replied, "We'll see".

I could go on forever ever or at least until I run out of ideas for little Juan, but I think you get the point.

And no, the point is not that the very old, wise man was indecisive. He was very old and wise because he knew that - what to some was a blessing but to others was a curse and to some what was a curse - was a blessing, (in disguise).

Old age tells you that.

You've lived long enough and seen enough to realize God uses all situations and all people to bring about what is needed.

He used a donkey, right?

So why shouldn't he use you or me to "bee" the miracle by making miracles happen to others.

Someone's doing it for us, right?

Another biblical principle in action that applies here is "you reap what you sow" - do good and good will come back to you.

If you *want good* in your life (reap), you first must *give good*, (plant, sow).

No plant - no harvest; or even worse - "sow bad - receive bad."

Life is circle and it's a circle because we are all connected to God, by God and with God. Whether you believe it or not - doesn't matter, it's just true.

But how about all those messages you delivered which were just your opinion - your idea, but you delivered them like they came from God. You delivered them like they were all-powerful, all-knowing and all-important, what about those?

How any times have you delivered one of them and got in the way of God?

What about messages delivered to you and you were too proud, stubborn, resentful or angry to listen. Or you hated the message or the messenger and your life got worse until God was finally able to flip the situation and get you on the right track.

How about those?

Doctors of all kinds working on any part of this human body of ours, lawyers, surgeons and nurses - *pay attention!*

Do you have any idea the power you have?

No, not in your "doctor, nursing, or legal skills" but in the mere fact that you are who you are.

That you represent "wisdom" in your profession.

People look to you as if you were a little bit of "God" here on earth, because you hold the outcome of their life in some way in your hands.

They look to *you* for their miracle.

Did you hear that?

Do you understand that?

Do you care about that? Or them?

Wake the heck up!

Quit thinking about golf, or money or the person you are

messing around with or your fake eye lashes. Really look and listen to the person who you are responsible for.

Yes, YOU are responsible for them - *because they have entrusted the outcome of their life with you. They are relying on you and your judgment.*

Are you 100% there when you talk with them, examine them and diagnose them?

Are you 100% there when you cleanse their wound that hurts like hell and has mutilated their weary body?

Are you 100% there when you sit behind your desk and tell them there's nothing that can be done or it will be another year before they see any money from their case all the while they are crying because they have ready lost their home and their mind?

Think!

And by the way, why did you want this power over someone else - was it for you?

If it was then you better get out of the way and let someone who is in it for "them" and not *themselves* take over.

Because you are a hindrance, you are a block to their miracle.

Give the miracle workers a chance to do their job and you go on and do something where it's all about you and not about other human beings. And then be grateful that God had someone deliver a wake-up call - deliver a wake-up package *to you* before you really did some irreversible damage.

Do you think I'm being too harsh? Do you think I'm being mean?

I really don't think so.

And the *important* word in this short sentence I just wrote – is think.

Think.

Okay, let's move on to another important word I have for you - obedience.

Whether you like this word or not doesn't matter.

What matters is treating others (and the package you are delivering to them), the way - *you* want to be treated and the way you want to be taken care of.

Here's my last brutally honest message - don't be a peace stealer.

That's right, a peace stealer. "What do I mean by that"?

I think you know what I mean.

Don't steal another person's peace of mind or their little "piece of heaven" here on earth. Accept that God has commissioned you to do this very important Proverb every day of your life and do it the right way - always.

He's actually created you to "be" this very important Proverb here on earth.

Why?

Because *you are him* here on earth, remember? He commissioned you to do this important Proverb every day of your life and do it the right way - always.

He's actually created you to "be" this very important Proverb here on earth.

Why? Because *you are him* here on earth, remember?

We've already discussed that. You have also heard that many times I am sure at church, on television, the radio or in discussions you've had. And I am sure God has told you it many times before - including as you were reading this book.

So, believe it. It's true. It's the truth.

I'm going to switch gears on you for a minute now.

Question - Have you ever had a great idea and then later you find out someone has done it and made lots of money or gained a lot of fame?

How did you feel? You were upset, right?

You felt like you had been cheated. Maybe you were envious of them or even secretly wished they'd lose that money or fame because it should have been yours.

Am I right?

Stop!

Don't blame them - you blew it.

You let it go to someone else who understood what to do with their gift-wrapped package - they were ready and their lamp was full of oil.

Inspirations are packages and they are blowing in the wind and they will fly past you if you don't catch them.

So, grab it, chase it and don't let it pass you buy - write it down as it is rushing past you and be grateful that it came your way.

Gratitude - remember?

...gratitude that you are in the flow because even though the creation is outside of you - the thought, the inspiration, is inside of you - the "perfect" mix of the two together.

It's God's package directly to you.

Yes, God's direct package to you without a secondary "FedEx" employee.

Because guess what?

This Proverb just doesn't mean that you are the one delivering the message initially. It also means that you can be the deliverer of "an aptly placed word" *after* - God sent the inspiration.

In this way, you are the sower. God has sent the package (message, idea, inspiration), and now *your part* is to sow it in fertile ground,

And to do that you must hoe, fertilize, water and weed.

God is using you as the gardener, as the farmer. He's sent the seed now it's your turn to sow - Seed for the Sower.

I understand this one pretty well. I lived in Statesboro, Georgia just a few miles away from Michael Guido and his ministry - Seed *for the Sower,* an amazing ministry and an amazing story.

Look it up it will bless you.

One last delivered package to you

Exciting work for you to do:

Journal for two days and look at the small and large things that are happening around and to you and recognize them as miracles.

Day #1

Day #2

_____

_____

_____

_____

_____

_____

_____

_____

_____

_____

_____

_____

_____

_____

Susan Farah

Now look back at those miracles – did they come from a negative experience or person or a positive? Hmmm…

_____

_____

_____

_____

_____

_____

_____

_____

_____

_____

_____

_____

_____

How about the miracles that have happened in your life?

_____

_____

_____

_____

_____

_____

_____

_____

_____

_____

_____

_____

_____

_____

_____

Chapter Eight

"...On Earth As It Is In Heaven"

What does that mean to you?

I know you have heard it for years and you've said it hundreds maybe even thousands of times, but did you understand it? Did you honestly realize what you were saying?

We know it must be important. It's part of the Lord's Prayer that Jesus gave on the Sermon on the Mount - famous, right?

But what does it *really mean - to you - today, in your life.*

I hope you have come to the realization that it means - anything that we can image that has been, can be or could be done in heaven - also can be on earth.

That we have the capability to do it right here on earth - on this planet, in our life and in this lifetime. The only one that can stop that from happening is us.

We are what we believe.

I never get tired of saying that.

Our belief is our reality. Whatever we believe is the truth that will be - we will make it so.

Our reality dictates our life.

If we believe we are happy - we are.

If we believe we are miserable - we are. And we will continue to be until we know that we know that we know we aren't - *only we can change that.*

So, what is your belief about heaven?

Do you even believe in heaven, I mean *really* believe there is a heaven?

And you better be honest with yourself because again, *what you believe is your reality and you - will have what you believe is true.*

The Lord's Prayer which you have said unthinkingly for years doesn't mean a "diddily squat" if you don't understand what you've been saying, and why you have been saying it!

Wake up!

Did you ever think "why" Jesus would have put that in the prayer that is supposed to be the most important prayer that we could ever pray to God?

The power is within you to be, to have and to do whatever you want.

But, you better focus on the right things and listen to the right voice. The voice who is trying to deliver an important package to you, a profound message that could change your life, the inspiration for the next part *of* the journey - *your life.*

This proverb that we have spent 100+ pages talking about so far is for you.

It was inspired and written for you - about you and because of you.

Let me share an interesting story I heard recently, actually it's *more* like an illustration. It goes something like this:

There *once* was a place *of* worship for all who were searching for truth.

This place had been around for many years and had stood the test of time; weather and the elements, wars and conflicts and loud discussions about who was right and who wasn't - what was right and what wasn't.

It stood when others had fallen or fallen by the wayside.

One day a man of some type of learning visited this place to discover why it had defied the odds and remained intact without change physically or philosophically.

He searched the place, talked to everyone, watched everything and then sat and thought until he came up with an answer. His answer, the reason this placed had survived, was the "holy" dance performed everyday by specially-trained worshippers.

The man just knew this dance was holy and "sacred" - it was spiritually uplifting, revered and ethereal.

He just had to bring this holy dance to his county, his place of worship. He asked the shaman, the wise sage and the guru for permission to do so.

Each smiled at him with wisdom in their eyes and replied, "Let it be as you want".

The man fervently watched every move the dancers made and wrote volumes. He even learned each movement himself making sure nothing was left out - not a movement, not a costume - not even an expression.

Finally, the day came when he left the place of worship and returned to his home. He taught his place of worship the holy dance and for the next year toured his entire country teaching this sacred dance. All the places of worship which learned the dance danced it every day just like the place of worship from which it originated.

Day after day in places of worship all across the man's country the holy dance was performed, more and more people were taught the dance and more and more people watched the dance until one day...

They stopped paying attention.

They stopped "seeing" the spirituality, so they stopped "feeling" what they presumed was "God". They got angry and lashed out at the man for wasting their time and making a "mockery" of them.

The man was bewildered.

What had he done that was so wrong?

Had he forgotten a step? Had he misread an expression?

He knew what he had to do - he must return to that place of worship and find out the truth, watch the holy dance again and get it right this time.

So, he made the long trip again and when he arrived at the place of worship he begged the shaman, the wise sage and the guru to help him.

"Please tell me what I have done wrong, what did I miss, what did I forget to teach them?" he asked.

Each one smiled at him with knowing and great compassion in their eyes as they summoned the dancers to dance.

As the man watched he became confused and then sat in horror as he watched a dance he had never seen before.

"This isn't the holy dance", he yelped.

He became agitated and then angrily accused them, "This isn't the dance I watched before that was performed every day in this place of worship".

They nodded in agreement then calmly the guru explained...

"The meaningless becomes holy - when the holy becomes meaningless."

When the holy becomes meaningless - you will make the meaningless become holy.

If you focus on an unimportant detail - that little thing that is different and build your doctrine and your life around it, you have missed the big picture - *what truly is holy.*

You have missed God.

That is why they changed the dance once it became ordinary - it became meaningless and worthless.

It never was about the dance.

The dance was worshipping God for - *His Holiness.*

He is holy - not the dance.

Think about it!

Your assignment: Do you understand the power is with you, the inspiration is with you? Journal for two days believing it.

Day #1

_____

_____

_____

_____

_____

_____

_____

_____

_____

_____

_____

_____

_____

_____

_____

Day #2

A Little Bit More...

If you're not creating your destroying, yourself and others.

Creating takes us out of ourselves so we forget to destroy.

Gratitude = Attitude. So be grateful.

Say thank you for everything – every day and you will have more to say "thank-you" about.

Surround everyone and everything with love.

Don't curse people or pray for that person to stop doing the thing you don't like - bless them.

Ask God to bless them and let God do his job - get out of his way.

Give God permission to do what he needs to.

Expect a miracle.

Ask. Believe. Receive.

Matthew 21:22 - "If you believe, you will receive whatever you ask for in prayer".

If you think life is negative and hard - you will get what you want.

Life is what you believe it is.

So, create your existence and enjoy it because - you are it. What's the dialog in your head saying to you?

If you think life is positive and good - you will get what you want.

Life is what you believe it is.

Find fun because it won't find you.

Whatever interests you take it seriously devote your passion to it.

Most people don't finish things - don't be one of them.

Our thoughts will equal the things in our life - we will make it so, "two for good, one for bad".

Our feelings, our passion is powerful. The more the feelings, the more the passion - the faster something will happen, (good or bad). Think about it.

Meditate on the good. Love, goodness, forgiveness = happiness, harmonious, bliss. God does not ask us to suffer or sacrifice - he asks us to be obedient.

It's not about what *we* want to give God or do for God – It's about what *God* is asking us to do.

it's about HIM not US!

If you truly love something you will endure almost anything- look at God, (and us).

Pay attention.

And don't whine. It's annoying. And it won't help.

Don't fight - focus on what you want not what you *don't* want or you'll get more of what you don't want.

Focus on the end product - your energy and creativity will elevate your passion until you create what you are focused on.

Creativity brings you into being - who you are. Who are you?

Experiment - for one whole day go around and sing everything, don't talk. Sing.

And guess what? No matter what happens you will be in a better mood. Singing comes from a different part of your brain.

Don't be afraid of the unknown of new things.

Pretend you are someone else - trick yourself into believing you are someone who is not afraid, someone who is brave - someone like "Indiana Jones" and just do it!

Tattoos (labels) are permanent - our bodies are temporary. Winston Churchill said, "*You* are creating your universe".

W.C. Fields said, "It's not what they call you - it's what you answer to."

Have a relationship with yourself - find out who you are. And when you do and if you like who you are - CELEBRATE.

If you don't - do something about it - CHANGE!

Be curious - never stop learning and searching. Never stop being curious.

Seamus Heaney, Nobel Laureate for poetry said, *"Keep dipping your bucket in the well until you have dipped into water - you'll have broken the skin on the part of yourself."*

Life is like a scavenger hunt.

If you want people in your life that are trustworthy - *be trustworthy.*

God is the Great I AM and "you" are the perfection of life... and his love.

Be in "awe" of you - amaze yourself every day.

You were created to be the best you can be.

To accomplish the best, give the best and receive the best.

Don't throw away your blessing!

Everything is already there waiting for someone - for *you* to unleash it. Give yourself permission to do it.

Validation = faith, trust, respect and love.

Go validate someone today – validate yourself today.

While we are here - things come and go. We come into the world with nothing, "no things". We leave the world with nothing, "no things".

The eternal part of us has nothing to do with things. Things are temporary - spirit is eternal. Therefore, we are spiritual beings.

The pure essence of you, the pure energy of you is eternal and spiritual. You are directly connected to your Creator.

The power is within you.

What are you going to do about it? What are you going to do with it?

Go walk on water.

"Bee" a pioneer.

About the Author

For over three decades Susan Farah has influenced others through her mentoring, teaching and writing. Her no-nonsense style and often wry sense of humor has brought her through many challenges of her own and helped others to do so, too.

She currently lives in Johnson City Tennessee with her spunky maltee-poo named Tillie, who loves to be called "silky smooth" even though she often looks like "scrappy coco".

Obviously, too many Adam Sandler movies have been watched.

Susan is thrilled to bring you another book which she hopes will inspire and challenge you - and ultimately change your life.